WE SHALL OVERCOME

THE MONTGOMERY BUS BOYCOTT

A PRIMARY SOURCE EXPLORATION OF THE PROTEST FOR EQUAL TREATMENT

by Allison Crotzer Kimmel

Consultant:
Lyde Cullen Sizer, PhD
Professor of U.S. Cultural and Intellectual History
Sarah Lawrence College
Bronxville, New York

CAPSTONE PRESS
a capstone imprint

Fact Finders Books are published by Capstone Press,
1710 Roe Crest Drive, North Mankato, Minnesota 56003
www.capstonepub.com

Library of Congress Cataloging-in-Publication Data
Kimmel, Allison Crotzer.
 The Montgomery Bus Boycott / Allison Crotzer Kimmel.
    pages cm.—(Fact finders. We shall overcome)
 Includes bibliographical references and index.
 Summary: "The Montgomery Bus Boycott began when Rosa Parks was arrested for refusing to give up her seat on
the bus. The campaign that followed was one of the most important protests against segregation in the United States.
The boycotters stood up for their beliefs. Explore the points of view of the boycotters and the people who opposed
them"—Provided by publisher.
 ISBN 978-1-4914-2043-0 (library binding)
 ISBN 978-1-4914-2218-2 (paperback)
 ISBN 978-1-4914-2233-5 (ebook PDF)
 1. Montgomery Bus Boycott, Montgomery, Ala., 1955–1956—Juvenile literature. 2. African Americans—Civil rights—
Alabama—Montgomery—History—20th century—Juvenile literature. 3. Civil rights movements—Alabama—
Montgomery—History—20th century—Juvenile literature. 4. Montgomery (Ala.)—Race relations—Juvenile
literature. I. Title.
 F334.M79N4533 2015
 323.1196'073076147—dc23   2014019815

Editorial Credits
Adrian Vigliano, editor; Cynthia Akiyoshi, designer; Wanda Winch, media researcher; Gene Bentdahl, production
specialist

Photo Credits
AP Images, 16, Gene Herrick, 17, 24, Horace Cort, 15; Corbis: Bettmann, 5, 25, Eudora Welty, 4, Hulton-Deutsch
Collection, 22; Birmingham Post-Herald, June 12, 1956, pg. 20, cover (background); Courtesy of Alean Bowser, 8;
Getty Images/The Life Images Collection/Don Cravens, cover, 11, 21, 26, Getty Images/The Life Images Collection/
Grey Villet, 18, 20, The Life Images Collection/Stan Wayman, 6, Time & Life Pictures/Myron Davis, 23, Tony Vaccaro,
7, UIG/Photo12, 10, UIG/Universal History Archive, 13, Library of Congress: Prints and Photographs Division, 9, 12,
19, 28; Newscom: Everett Collection, 27

Author's Dedication
For my grandparents, Charlie, Mary, Tim, and Eleda, who taught me the importance of history.

Printed in Canada.
092014   008478FRS15

TABLE OF CONTENTS

A NOTE ABOUT PRIMARY SOURCES

Primary sources are newspaper articles, photographs, speeches, or other documents that were created during an event. They are great ways to see how people spoke and felt during that time. You'll find primary sources from the time of the Montgomery Bus Boycott throughout this book. Within the text, these primary sources are colored blue and set in italic type.

Chapter One

SETTING THE STAGE FOR MONTGOMERY

As the Civil War (1861–1865) was coming to an end, the 13th Amendment to the U.S. Constitution **abolished** slavery. In 1868 the 14th Amendment promised equal rights to all citizens. But new Amendments could not change the attitudes of people who had long believed blacks were lesser people than whites.

In 1896 the Supreme Court said a law giving *"equal but separate accommodations for the white, and colored, races"* was constitutional. This kept **segregation** legal. Many new "Jim Crow" laws sprang up all over the South.

▶ Black or "colored" people were treated like second-class citizens under Jim Crow laws.

abolish—to put an end to something officially

segregate—to keep people of different races apart in public places

Segregation shaped all interactions between black and white people.

FOR COLORED ONLY

Jim Crow laws separated black people from white people. Black people had to sit in the backs of buses and trains. They had to eat separately from white people in restaurants. Black children had to go to different schools than white children. Facilities for black people were often in poor condition.

There were also unwritten rules of the Jim Crow South. Black people had to address all whites as "sir" or "ma'am." Blacks stepped off the curbs of sidewalks to let whites pass. Disobeying these rules could cause a black person to be beaten or killed.

FACT

Jim Crow was a character in traveling shows in the early 1830s and 1840s. The character made fun of blacks. The character's name came to be used to describe segregation laws.

Chapter Two

MONTGOMERY BUSES AND SEGREGATION

In 1955 in Alabama's state capital, Montgomery, 40 percent of the residents were black. Like many black Southerners, a large number of black Montgomerians worked in **domestic** jobs. They were nannies or cooks in people's homes. Most did not earn enough money to buy a vehicle, so they relied on buses. Between 75 and 80 percent of Montgomery's bus riders at this time were black domestic workers.

Montgomery's only bus company was Montgomery City Lines. The company's rules said the 10 front seats in any bus were for whites. The rear 10 seats were for blacks. The middle 16 seats were usually for any passenger, black or white.

▶ Bus segregation rules were designed to favor white passengers.

509
NO SMOKING

COLORED SEAT FROM REAR

COLLINS AVE.
TO HOLLYWOOD

▶ Because bus drivers had police power, disobedient passengers could be fined or arrested.

The Montgomery city code supported the bus company's rules. The code said, *"it shall be unlawful for any passenger to refuse or fail to take a seat among those assigned to the race to which he belongs ..."* The city code also gave each bus driver *"the powers of a police officer of the city."* This meant that passengers had to follow a bus driver's orders.

domestic—relating to the household or family

Segregation made riding a bus in Montgomery frustrating and unfair for black people. Blacks had to pay their fare at the front of the bus, exit, and re-enter from the rear. Some drivers drove away without letting black passengers re-enter the bus after paying.

On the bus everything worked in favor of white riders. Drivers forced black passengers to stay away from whites. A whole row of black people could be moved to let one white passenger sit. Some drivers even abused black riders by slamming on the brakes to knock down standing passengers. Black Montgomerians complained of the unfair treatment, but nothing changed.

▶ Fifteen-year-old Claudette Colvin was the first of several women who challenged bus segregation in Montgomery.

E.D. Nixon

Edgar Daniel Nixon was president of the Montgomery and Alabama chapters of the National Association for the Advancement of Colored People (NAACP). He had long believed blacks deserved equal rights. Nixon was also president of the first successful black workers' union in Alabama. He fought against the Jim Crow system and was a well-respected black community leader in Montgomery.

Claudette Colvin was just 15 on March 2, 1955, when she was pulled from a bus and handcuffed. She had refused to give her seat to a white woman, saying: *"It's my constitutional right to sit here as much as that lady. I paid my fare ..."* This event started talk of a bus **boycott**, but black community activist E.D. Nixon felt the time was not right.

boycott—to refuse to take part in something as a way of making a protest

Chapter Three

ONE BUS, TWO LIVES

Rosa Parks was born in 1913 and grew up in Montgomery. She knew firsthand the **discrimination** black citizens faced. Once when she was a child she was walking through a white neighborhood. A white boy tried to knock her off the sidewalk. She later recalled, *"I turned around and pushed him. A white woman was standing not too far from us. She turned out to be his mother, because she said she could put me so far in jail that I never would get out again for pushing her child."*

▶ As a child, Parks lived with her grandparents—both former slaves—in Alabama. Her grandparents believed strongly in racial equality.

discriminate—to treat people unfairly because of their skin color or class

Parks was a civil rights activist long before she became famous. She joined the NAACP in 1943, working as a youth leader as well as Nixon's secretary.

In 1955 Parks was a 42-year-old seamstress whom many described as *"a real lady."* She had previously worked with E.D. Nixon as secretary for the Montgomery NAACP. She also knew that many blacks had been beaten or killed in Montgomery for the slightest act of defiance.

Parks learned what to do if ever she were put in a situation where she was pitted against a white citizen. She knew not to shout or struggle physically. Her time with Nixon at the NAACP taught her to sit in quiet defiance.

A Taste of Integration

Rosa Parks experienced **integration** when working at Montgomery's Maxwell Field Army Air Force Base in 1941. President Roosevelt did not allow segregation on military bases. She said, *"You might just say Maxwell opened my eyes up. It was an alternative reality to the ugly policies of Jim Crow."*

integrate—to bring people of different races together in schools and other public places

On December 1, 1955, Parks boarded a bus, sitting in the row directly behind the white seats. The bus began to fill. When a white man boarded, the bus driver asked Parks and three other black people to move. Parks recognized the driver as the man who had once driven off without her after she'd paid her fare.

None of the black passengers moved. The bus driver, James Blake, said, *"Y'all better make it light on yourselves and let me have those seats."* The other three blacks moved, but Parks said, *"No. I'm tired of being treated like a second-class citizen."*

▶ Parks later spoke about the incident that led to her arrest. *"I had decided that I would have to know once and for all what rights I had as a human being and a citizen even in Montgomery, Alabama."*

▶ Parks was taken to jail for her actions on the bus. Later, many people began calling her "the mother of the civil rights movement."

Instead of getting up, Parks slid to the window seat. She looked at the movie theater outside. The bus driver threatened to have her arrested. Parks said, *"You may do that."*

The police were sent to arrest Parks. She asked them, *"Why do you all push us around?"*

One officer shrugged as he responded, *"I don't know, but the law is the law, and you're under arrest."*

A Man Who Had His Orders

Blake later explained his encounter with Parks by saying, *"I had my orders. I had police powers—any driver for the city did. So the bus filled up and a white man got on and she had his seat and I told her to move back and she wouldn't do it ... I got my supervisor on the line. He said, 'Did you warn her, Jim?' I said, 'I warned her.' And he said, and I remember it just like I'm standing here, 'Well then, Jim, you do it, you got to exercise your powers and put her off, hear?' And that's just what I did."*

▶ Public buses were an important form of transportation for Montgomery's black population.

Blake claimed that blacks began calling his house to make threats. Years later he said, *"I wasn't trying to do anything to that Parks woman except do my job. She was in violation of the city codes. What was I supposed to do?"*

Chapter Four

381 DAYS TO VICTORY

On the evening of December 1, white attorney Clifford Durr and E.D. Nixon bailed Rosa Parks out of jail. Nixon helped plan a one-day bus boycott to protest Parks' arrest. He also convinced Rev. Dr. Martin Luther King, Jr. to join the boycott. King was new to Montgomery but had become a leader in the black community as pastor of the Dexter Avenue Baptist Church.

▶ Nixon (center) convinced Parks that her experience could be used to challenge Montgomery's bus segregation.

► Hundreds of supporters cheered on Parks as she arrived at the courthouse for her trial on Monday, December 5, 1955.

College professor Jo Ann Robinson helped organize the boycott. She wrote a leaflet asking blacks to join the planned one-day boycott. Robinson and a few others distributed more than 50,000 copies around Montgomery. She wrote in the leaflet, *"Another Negro woman has been arrested and thrown in jail because she refused to get up out of her seat on the bus for a white person to sit down ... This has to be stopped. Negroes have rights, too, for if Negroes did not ride the buses, they could not operate ... The next time it may be you, or your daughter, or mother ... We are, therefore, asking every Negro to stay off the buses Monday in protest of the arrest and trial ... Don't ride the buses to work, to town, to school, or anywhere on Monday."*

The Fight Begins

On Monday December 5, 1955, Rosa Parks was tried and convicted in less than five minutes. She was fined $10 plus $4 in court costs. For many black Montgomerians this was a week's wages. Maids earned $10 and factory workers earned around $20 weekly. Parks refused to pay the fine, saying the segregation laws were illegal.

Many black Montgomerians stood strong like Parks. They did as Jo Ann Robinson had asked and did not ride the buses. The Montgomery Bus Boycott had officially begun.

▶ Montgomery's buses were nearly empty when thousands of black commuters boycotted.

► King became a nationally known civil rights leader during the boycott.

That night the Montgomery Improvement Association (MIA) held a public meeting. The MIA had been formed earlier that day with King as its president. Its purpose was to support the efforts of the boycott. King spoke to the large crowd gathered at the meeting. He explained that he did not support the use of violence, saying, *"I want it to be known throughout Montgomery and throughout this nation that we are Christian people ... The only weapon that we have in our hands this evening is the weapon of protest."*

FACT

The MIA meeting was held at the Holt Street Baptist Church in a working-class area of Montgomery. Several thousand people packed the church. It was so crowded it took King about 15 minutes to get through the crowd so he could speak.

Organizing the Boycott

Boycott supporters began to work together to find ways to replace the buses. Black-owned taxi companies had existed in Montgomery before the boycott. But most black Montgomerians did not ride taxis because taxi fares were much more expensive than the 10-cent bus fare. To support the boycott, black-owned taxi companies lowered their fares to 10 cents. But city officials quickly began enforcing a previously ignored **ordinance** that set minimum fares at 45 cents.

MIA leaders organized a carpool system for the boycotters to use instead of buses. The carpool system started on December 13. Some churches supported the MIA's effort and bought vehicles for the carpool. Many people, even some white citizens, drove black Montgomerians to and from work.

▶ Some boycotters walked as far as 20 miles (32 kilometers) on their way to work.

ordinance—a law made by a city government

▶ The MIA's carpool ran efficiently with many areas for boycotters to be picked up and dropped off. Police often ticketed or arrested carpool drivers for minor traffic violations.

The spirit of the protest swept through the black community. Some boycotters rode bicycles. Many simply walked. One elderly woman said, *"I'm not walking for myself. I'm walking for my children and my grandchildren."*

Robert Graetz

Robert Graetz was the white pastor of the mostly black Trinity Lutheran Church in Montgomery. He joined the executive committee of the MIA and helped coordinate volunteers for the carpool. Like other boycott leaders, Graetz and his family were violently attacked by hate groups. He said later, *"People either loved us or hated us. Few showed indifference. People often said we had courage. There were times when I was scared to death."*

Violence

Many white citizens were strongly opposed to the boycott. They wanted to protect the system of segregation. One told King, *"Over the years we have had such peaceful and harmonious race relations here. Why have you and your associates come in to destroy this long tradition?"*

Other people responded violently to the boycott. King, Nixon, and Graetz's homes were all bombed. King received postcards that said, *"get out of town or else."* The cards were signed *"KKK"* for the Ku Klux Klan, a hate group.

► Hate groups such as the Ku Klux Klan had a history of using threats and violence to enforce segregation.

The local WCC held meetings in response to the bus boycott. After Mayor Gayle joined the group he said, *"I think every right-thinking white person in Montgomery, Alabama, and the South should do the same. We must make certain that Negroes are not allowed to force their demands on us."*

The boycotters faced opposition from the local government too. Under Mayor William A. Gayle's leadership, black citizens were increasingly abused. Many were arrested in an effort to bully them away from the boycott. Gayle was a member of the local White Citizens' Council (WCC). WCC groups were determined to keep racial segregation throughout the South. Gayle said white Montgomerians *"don't care whether a Negro ever rides a bus again if it means that the social fabric of our community is to be destroyed so that the Negroes will start riding buses again."*

Montgomery city officials, the bus company, and the MIA were locked in a battle that would last well over a year.

Mayor Gayle said the city council would do everything it could to keep racial segregation. He said, *"There seems to be a belief on the part of the Negroes that they have the white people hemmed up in a corner and they are not going to give an inch until they can force the white people of our community to submit to their demands—in fact, swallow all of them."*

Police Commissioner Clyde Sellers said, *"This boycott has done damage that can never be repaired. It has done more harm to the [Negro] cause than anything else."* Sellers and the other Montgomery City Commissioners also joined the WCC.

► Gayle refused to negotiate with the MIA and said that any bus driver who disobeyed segregation laws would be arrested.

24

▶ Clyde Sellers (far right) stood beside King outside of King's home after it was bombed. Sellers told King, *"I do not agree with you in your beliefs, but I will do everything within my power to defend you against such acts as this."*

The boycott continued to put pressure on Montgomery in many ways. Shops and other businesses lost thousands of dollars as fewer blacks came downtown. Many shopkeepers did not want integration, but they wanted the boycott to end because it was bad for business. It was estimated that the boycott cost Montgomery City Lines 65 percent of its business. It lost an average of $3,500 each day—about $1 million by the end of the boycott.

Victory

The MIA filed a federal lawsuit, *Browder v. Gayle*, challenging bus segregation laws. On June 5, 1956, a federal court said segregated bus seating was unconstitutional. The Supreme Court agreed on November 13. City and state governments appealed the ruling, but the Supreme Court rejected the appeals. Montgomery city buses could no longer be segregated.

▶ Jo Ann Robinson (not pictured) wrote about increased police pressure during the boycott: *"Hundreds of Black motorists were stopped, searched, questioned and given tickets for traffic violations. I myself received 17 traffic tickets for all kinds of trumped-up charges."*

▶ King (2nd row on left) joined a group of black and white boycott leaders on a Montgomery City Lines bus on December 21, 1956. They rode in the part of the bus that had once been reserved for whites.

MIA leaders Ralph Abernathy, Nixon, and King rode on the first integrated bus. Many reporters watched. The bus driver first spoke to King. *"I believe you are Reverend King?"* When King answered that he was, the driver said simply, *"We are glad to have you with us this morning."*

Chapter Five

THE BOYCOTT THAT STARTED THE CIVIL RIGHTS MOVEMENT

The success of the boycott also had its costs. Rosa Parks and her husband, Raymond, had to leave Alabama in 1957 because of death threats. Parks continued to work for civil rights the rest of her life. James Blake retired from the Montgomery City Lines in 1974. Though many who knew Blake defended him, his part in the incident followed him for life.

▶ After the boycott Parks said, *"I had no idea when I refused to give up my seat on that Montgomery bus that my small action would help put an end to the segregation laws in the South."*

King's Church

King's Dexter Avenue Baptist Church was only steps away from the Alabama State Capitol. The capitol building was where Jefferson Davis took the oath of office as president of the Confederate States during the Civil War. During the Civil War, Montgomery became known as the "Cradle of the Confederacy." Because of the bus boycott, it is also known as the "birthplace of the civil rights movement."

The Montgomery bus boycott was the first large protest against segregation. It proved change could happen through nonviolence. It encouraged other black communities in the South to protest racial discrimination peacefully. The boycott also made King a nationally known civil rights leader. King later remembered the boycott, saying, *"The story of Montgomery is the story of 50,000 Negroes who are tired of injustices and oppression, and who are willing to substitute tired feet for tired souls, and walk and walk until the walls of injustice are crushed by the battering rams of historical necessity."*

Selected Bibliography

Adler, Margot. "Before Rosa Parks, There Was Claudette Colvin." NPR, March 15, 2009. http://www.npr.org/templates/story/story.php?storyId=101719889

Branch, Taylor. *The King Years: Historic Moments in the Civil Rights Movement*. New York: Simon & Schuster, 2013.

Brinkley, Douglas. *Rosa Parks*. New York: Viking, 2000.

Haygood, Wil. "The Thread That Unraveled Segregation" *The Washington Post*, October 26, 2005. http://www.washingtonpost.com/wp-dyn/content/article/2005/10/25/AR2005102501700.html

Hendrickson, Paul. "Montgomery 1955: The Supporting Actors in the Historic Bus Boycott." *The Washington Post*, July 24, 1989. http://www.highbeam.com/doc/1P2-1202889.html

"James F. Blake Obituary." *The Guardian*, March 26, 2002. http://www.theguardian.com/news/2002/mar/27/guardianobituaries

King, Martin Luther, Jr. *Stride Toward Freedom: The Montgomery Story*. New York: Harper, 1958.

McGrew, Jannell. "Rev. Robert Graetz." *The Montgomery Advertiser*. http://www.montgomeryboycott.com/rev-robert-graetz

"The Montgomery Bus Boycott: They Changed the World." *The Montgomery Advertiser*. http://www.montgomeryboycott.com/overview

"Montgomery City Code." IIT Chicago Kent Law Library Blog, February 2, 2013. http://blogs.kentlaw.iit.edu/library/exhibits/montgomery-1955/images-documents/montgomery-city-code/

Phibbs, Cheryl. *The Montgomery Bus Boycott: A History and Reference Guide*. Santa Barbara, Calif.: Greenwood, 2009.

Glossary

abolish (uh-BOL-ish)—to put an end to something officially

boycott (BOY-kot)—to refuse to take part in something as a way of making a protest

discriminate (dis-KRI-muh-nayt)—to treat people unfairly because of their skin color or class

domestic (duh-MES-tik)—relating to the household or family

integrate (IN-tuh-grate)—to bring people of different races together in schools and other public places

ordinance (OR-din-anss)—a law made by a city government

segregate (SEG-ruh-gate)—to keep people of different races apart in schools and other public places

Critical Thinking Using the Common Core

1. Many protesters were ticketed, arrested, or attacked during the boycott. Discuss some of the reasons why people might accept great risks to take a stand against segregation. (Key Ideas and Details)

2. Why do you think some people were so opposed to integrating the buses? Discuss the different reactions these people had. Were their reactions justified? Support your answer with examples from the text and other sources. (Integration of Knowledge and Ideas)

Internet Sites

FactHound offers a safe, fun way to find Internet sites related to this book.
All of the sites on FactHound have been researched by our staff.

Here's all you do:
Visit *www.facthound.com*
Type in this code: 9781491420430

 Check out projects, games and lots more at
www.capstonekids.com

Index